Olga's Story: Stormy Sea

by

Olga Wilmes

The contents of this work, including, but not limited to, the accuracy of events, people, and places depicted; opinions expressed; permission to use previously published materials included; and any advice given or actions advocated are solely the responsibility of the author, who assumes all liability for said work and indemnifies the publisher against any claims stemming from publication of the work.

All Rights Reserved
Copyright © 2023 by Olga Wilmes

No part of this book may be reproduced or transmitted, downloaded, distributed, reverse engineered, or stored in or introduced into any information storage and retrieval system, in any form or by any means, including photocopying and recording, whether electronic or mechanical, now known or hereinafter invented without permission in writing from the publisher.

Dorrance Publishing Co
585 Alpha Drive
Pittsburgh, PA 15238
Visit our website at *www.dorrancebookstore.com*

ISBN: 978-1-6386-7132-9
eISBN: 978-1-6386-7947-9

Dedication

To my parents
Johan Friesen
Justina Friesen

INTRODUCTION

THE FIRST MENNONITES CAME from Prussia (now Poland) from the area around Danzig, in the year, 1789. This was the year of the beginning of the French revolution. The Polish people were in the unfortunate position of being partitioned in these years between three larger empires, Russia, Austria and Prussia.

The area around the mouth of the Vistula River, where the Mennonites had settled, fell into the hands of Frederick the Great. Poland had been a homeland for this group of Mennonites ever since the second half of the 16th century; they had fled there from Holland as Anabaptists had been persecuted for their faith.

Frederick the Great, began to draft their men into his Prussian army (Prussia is Poland now). He started to take control of the Scrod's, so they began to look for another place to settle down.

These Mennonites were happy to accept Katherine's invitation to Russia where they were promised freedom of religion, and would not have to serve in the military and have plenty and land to farm.

One thing that bothered the spiritual leaders was that they were not to talk to the Russian people about their faith.

The first settlers came to the southern Ukraine about 200 miles north of the Crimea and the Black Sea. This was the colony called Chortitza. The river that flowed through this colony, flowed into the Dnieper River which flows into the Black Sea. This colony had about nineteen villages of 400,000 acres all together. About one hundred miles southeast of this colony, a second Colony was founded called Molotschna Colony, in the beginning of the 1830's. The Molotschna Colony had sixty villages. Later on this Colony was divided up in two parts, one half had Halbstadt as their administrative center and the other part had Gnadenfeld as their center.

Chapter 1
RUSSIA: BEGINNINGS

"Give me, my son, your heart"—Proverbs 23:26

As the nineteenth century drew to a close, imperialism flourished in many parts of the world. Whether beneath the flags of Queen Victoria, the czars, or other European monarchs, the people of the earth were being subjugated supposedly for their own good, and learning the ways of "better" civilization and culture. Far away from the great centers of civilization, the small religious group called Mennonites had virtually established its own little kingdom on the steppes of Russia. For over a century they had pursued a peaceful existence in their own colonies and villages and established a unique way of life—Germanic and radically Protestant.

My name is Mrs. Olga Wilmes. I was born in south Russia, which is now known as the Ukraine. My maiden name was Olga Friesen. I was one of eight girls born to Johan and Justina Friesen. I was the second youngest in my family. This is my story.

My forefathers emigrated from the Netherlands (Holland). They immigrated to Russia when a person could live under freedom. The Czar of Russia promised our forefathers freedom of religion and that we could live there peacefully as German people.

My mother was born on December 29, 1898, in a small village called Furstenwerder in the Colony of Moloschna located in the Ukraine, a part of Russia which can be compared to a state in the United States of America. It was a very big state, much bigger than New York state.

My father was born on April 24, 1894, and he married my mother on May 25, 1921. My father's name is Johan Friesen and my mother's name was Tascha Braun. After they married, they lived in a village called Petershagen. This is a German name. My father was the youngest child born to his parents. Both his parents died of typhoid fever during a plague. At that time they did not have the medicine to cure the disease. Five of my father's family died from typhoid in one year. Also during that year one of his brothers was murdered. It was a very difficult time for my father, to lose five of his loved ones in one year. It was after his parents had died that he married my mother.

My parents lived in Petershagen for four years and two of my oldest sisters were born there. They were named Tascha and Anita. After that time, they moved to the village of Alexanderwohl (also a German name). Here six more of us were born. They named us Helga, Margaret, Sonja, Magdalen, Olga, and Irma. We lived in one of three German Mennonite colonies, Old Colony, Sagradowka, and Meloschna, is where we lived.

A revolution broke out in Russia and the last czar and his entire family were killed. The Russian Communists fought to overthrow the government and gain control. During this revolution the Communists became known as "Reds" and the opposing troops were known as the "Whites." The reds were atheists and the Whites were known as "conservatives."

The last czar was killed in the year of 1917. He was riding with his family on a train and was surrounded by his bodyguards. The Communists overpowered the train and the czar's bodyguards. They killed the czar and his family.

At this time, the Communists released many hard-core criminals from the Russian prisons. Many of them had been sentenced to prison because they had murdered people. These released prisoners killed all the prison guards and then formed a group of terrorists. They were led by a notorious murderer whose name was Nestor Machno.

These terrorists armed themselves with weapons and traveled all over Russia. Whenever they came to a village, they demanded any food available and slaughtered anyone who tried to oppose them. They had absolutely no regard for human life. I have a small book which records the slaughter of a whole German village. Every man, woman, and child was killed and placed in a massive grave in which 58 people are buried. It was a very terrible time for all of us. We never knew where these terrorists were or when they might pass through our village. This happened before I was born, in 1918–19. I had horrible nightmares about people having their heads cut off. The terrorists continued their raids and massacres for three years, leaving many people without anything left of their food or possessions. They often hacked people to pieces with their machetes.

After two years of fighting between the Red Army and the White Army, the Red Army won the war and took control of Russia. As soon as they were in power, they went after the terrorists and killed all of them except the leader—Machno, who escaped to France. He lived there until he died some years later, an alcoholic and diseased man. We were glad that the Communists killed the terrorists. Now Russia was under Communist rule. The person in control of Russia was Lenin. Things became increasingly difficult for us. They made Sunday another working day. All churches were closed and became barns for animals. They took our animals from us—all our cows, horses, pigs, chickens—leaving us with no food. Our villages were turned into big Kolchozes (working places) where everyone would come to work together for the government. The government now owned everything which belonged to us and also owned us. They allowed each family to own one cow for milk but eventually they took that away from us too.

It was reported that Lenin died of a heart attack. We believe that others who wanted to control Russia poisoned him. Things were very difficult under his rule but were even more difficult under the rule of Stalin, who now was the leader of Russia. He once took a chicken and pulled out all its feathers. It was so cold it rubbed and pushed close to his feet. Stalin said to his generals and officers, "Look. Do you see this chicken? It does not leave my feet. That's what we will do with all the people in our land. We will take everything away from them and they will be mine." That is exactly what he did to us.

We lived in one of three German Mennonite colonies in which were about thirty small villages. Each village had one long street lined on both sides with homes with a little bit of land. Most homes had areas to farm. The area we farmed was surrounded by a beautiful white fence. We had a fruit garden on one side of our house. It was a big and beautiful fruit garden. We had everything we needed for food on our farm. Any other supplies were purchased at the one store in our colony. There we could buy spices for baking and cooking and fabric to make clothes.

The hardships that took over us in Russia are very difficult to share. Everything was taken from us. The Communists put a high fence around our fruit orchard and forbade us to take any fruit from it. They also took the last cows from all the people. They removed everything we had in our homes, even to the last handful of flour in our flour bins. They removed all the grain stored in our barns, and piled it up outside of our villages, and let it rot. Our land for farming was a few miles away from our village. We did not need much farmland. The soil was extremely rich and highly productive. This area had become known as "the Breadbasket of the World." Now it no longer was ours to farm and produce the food we needed to live.

We were left with nothing at all to eat. A terrible famine took over our land. People were dying all around us. My grandmother and Aunt Helga were put out on the street with only the clothes they were wearing. They had nothing else. Everything they had, including their home was taken from them and they were forced to live in the streets. At night my parents took them into our home, to share what little food we had and give them a place to sleep. My parents did this at great risk. Had they been caught by the Secret Police, they would have been sent to Siberia to work in a labor camp and we never would have seen them again. Then the Communists would have raised us children. God was protecting our family.

When my sister Margaret was born, my mother had no clothing for her because everything had been taken away from us. Each of us was allowed only one set of clothing. My mother took an old shirt of my father's and cut it into a few pieces. This became the clothing for her newborn baby. A portion of that shirt became the baby's diaper. At night, my mother would wash the pieces of the shirt and dry it in front of the wooden stove while the baby was asleep.

We had no central heat in our homes. Every morning my mother got up very early to get some wood which she gathered from outside and put it into a stove to make a little fire in our kitchen. Only the kitchen had some heat. My little sister Margaret as a baby was very ill because we had no food to eat and my mother had no milk to breast-feed her. My mother was very concerned that Margaret would die. She was certain Margaret would not live. But the Lord God gave us grace again and brought my sister through that difficult time.

No longer were we given the freedom promised to my grandparents. No longer could we worship God or read His Word. No longer could we freely pray without fear of being caught. When my parents would pray in the evening and read the Bible, they would hang a thick blanket in front of every window and close every door. Then they prayed and read God's Word very quietly. The Secret Police prowled our neighborhoods in search of anyone who dared to pray or read the Bible. It was not possible to identify them because they did not dress in uniforms. No one really knew who they were. All our Bibles had to be hidden and any Scripture verses removed from our walls. Children were questioned in school about their parents. They were asked if their parents prayed or read the Bible. We could trust no one!

Some parents were removed from their homes because they were discovered reading God's Word and praying with their children. They were sent to Siberia to work in Communist labor camps. The children in those homes were raised in a Communist camp where they were brainwashed and Communism was forced into their minds and hearts.

The new leader of Russia, Stalin, commanded his Secret Police to control what was being read in the schools. They convinced the students that Stalin was their god by making holes in the schoolroom ceilings and dropping candy through the holes. The teachers informed the students that it was Stalin, their god, who was giving them candy. Children had to attend school on Sundays and even Easter and Christmas. Both our parents were forced to work seven day a week. My mother did her housework and took care of all of us in the evenings and well into the night. Sometimes she was so tired that she would fall asleep while she cooked our dinner or did our wash.

My parents and two of my oldest sisters had to work in the Kolchoz where everybody in our village were forced to work together. Only those who worked would get some food to eat. They received some potatoes, one cup of milk, a small portion of flour and a small piece of bread. That was the entire wages for seven days of hard work.

Two of my uncles were taken away by the Communists. My uncle Jake, my mother's brother, was taken and also my uncle Abraham, my aunt Maria's husband. Uncle Abraham was taken away and questioned twice by the Secret Police and released. During this time four of the six children born to my aunt and uncle died. After they took Uncle Abraham the second time, Aunt Maria died because of the hardships we had to suffer. We had very little if any food and no medicine and no doctors to care for the sick because they had all been taken away. There was absolutely no help or care for Aunt Maria. The Secret Police again took Uncle Abraham and this time he did not return. They tortured him to death. I am so thankful to God that my parents and aunts and uncles were all believers in our Lord Jesus Christ. I will see them in heaven some day.

Chapter 2
Surviving

My mother's youngest sister, Tina, often babysat for my mother while she worked on the Kolchoz. My mother promised her sister, Aunt Tina, that someday she would return the kindness by having one of us baby-sit for her when she married and had children of her own. Aunt Tina did marry but because of the difficult times we had to endure she and her family moved to Kazakhstan, which was a great distance from us, about 3,000 kilometers.

My father decided that in order to keep us alive he would go to Kazakhstan where my Aunt Tina lived. Perhaps he could get some kind of work there so that we would have bread for our family, so he left in search of work. He did find some work for a small sum of money and sent my mother some food to keep us alive. He remained there for about six months and then returned home.

The Communists realized that too many children had died and if this continued they would have no young people for their army. They gave an allotment of money to each family who had seven or more children. My parents received some money (2,000 rubles per child) for me because I was the seventh child and for my sister Irma who was the eighth child.

Chapter 3
The War Years

Now World War II spread over Europe—the War Years. Just before the German army came into Russia, the Communists removed all men from 16 to 65 years of age from our villages. Because the German army advanced so suddenly, the Russians did not have enough time to ship the women and children to Siberia also. All the women and their children were left behind. My father was among those who were taken. Many families watched as their husbands, sons, fathers, and brothers were forced to leave their families behind. It was very difficult for the women who were left to care for their families without their husbands.

My father and two other men from our village escaped from the Communists. They came back to our village and hid for three months. My father was so afraid that they would find him that he turned himself in and was taken away again. If he had waited one more month, he would have been there when the German army came and might have been with us. It is quite possible, though, that he would have had to fight for the Germans against the Russians and might have been killed anyway.

When the men and boys were taken they drove them for about a hundred kilometers and then ordered them out of the trucks in which they were riding. They were forced to walk hundreds of miles. The weather was extremely cold. Some did not make it because they had no food. The rest were herded inside freight trains, which had no heat. This was the middle of winter. After they rode those trains for many hours they were ordered outside into the snow and ordered to remove all their clothing except for their underwear. They were permitted to keep that. Then they were ordered to sit in the snow for a long time. Many of those men never got up because they froze to death. Those who were left were ordered back into the train and were sent to the Siberian forest to a labor camp. One of those men who died in the snow could have been my father. We do not know what happened to him. My father either died or was killed. The reason for ordering those men to die in the snow was that they did not want to waste bullets in killing them. Freezing them to death seemed to be a better way to kill them.

We realize that when someone who does not know and serve God and is not saved gets into power he can be very cold and cruel to those who are under him. It is important to seek the Lord before it is too late. Russia and Germany had been at war for some time now. Since all the men and boys had been sent to Siberia the only problem that remained was the women and children. Because there were so many of us, they decided that it would be impossible to use weapons to kill us. They had another plan for us, although we did not know that at this time. They planned to take us all and ship all of us to one place where we would be killed. I remember my mother getting seven of us ready. My sister Helga, who was twelve years old, was not with us at this time because of my mother's promise to Aunt Tina. She was with her and her family in Kazsakhstan to help her. She had gone to live with her about two months before my father was taken away. She was with Aunt Tina only a few weeks when the war between Russia and Germany began. Since our government forbid any travel, Helga could not return to us. It was many years before we heard from her again.

Chapter 4
Sent to be Killed

Now the remaining seven of us and my mother were told to get ready to leave our home. We were driven by horse wagon to Tackmack, a city about 100 kilometers away from our villages. All the women and children from the three German colonies, a great number, were driven to Tackmack where there were three big storage houses for grain. All of us were ordered inside. We were informed that the German army wanted to kill us. They told us that the German bomber would pass over the grain-storage houses three times and on the third pass he would drop his bomb on us. They said that if a fire resulted, they would open the doors of the barns and we could get out.

The Communists locked the doors from the outside and we were left to wait for the passing of the German bomber. My youngest sister Irma and I had eye infections. Mother had nothing to help us. But my mother was a praying mother. She trusted the Lord in every situation and God used a very simple method to wipe our eyes and we got better. Many people were in very poor health. There were no toilets in these barns. Mothers had taken the children's potties and this is what we used.

Small groups of mothers and families huddled together and remained very quiet. No one said a word and no child cried as we listened and we heard the plane coming. We listened as the plane came closer and flew over us. Then in silence, we listened as the plane passed over the barn again. Then we heard it coming for the third time. No one said a word. Everyone was quiet but all were praying in their hearts to God.

We heard a terrible explosion and all of a sudden the doors were open and we could get out.

We realized that the Russian Communists had not opened the doors. They had left long before the bombs were dropped, in fear of their own lives. They had lied to us when they said they would open the doors. God was in charge. He had protected us. Perhaps He sent His angels to open those doors or used someone who was against the Communists to let us out.

Every mother gathered her children and ran. My mother carried Irma, my oldest sister took me, and the other sisters ran behind us. As we looked back, all three grain barns were one big flame of fire. No one was killed—not one mother and not one child. All of us survived. God again, in His grace, protected us. Some of us suffered minor injuries from the falling roof tiles, but no injury was serious.

We were told we could return back home. We walked the hundred kilometers back to our villages. We allowed distance between each family group so that we would not be noticed by the Russian people who lived in the area through which we had to pass. We were afraid that they, too, might harm us.

God is good. It is amazing that He even used some Russian terrorists to take pity on us. They bandaged my sisters' bleeding heads and gave us some food to eat.

We later found out that the pilot who flew that plane was not a German, but was a Russian who had been ordered by the Communist government to have us all killed. When he realized what his assignment was, he determined not to kill those women and children. Proverbs 16:7 says: "When a man's ways please the Lord, He makes even his enemies to be at peace with him." That Russian pilot had compassion on us. What mankind means for evil, God can bring something good. God protected our lives so many times. I am thankful to God for His Grace.

My mother had three Bible verses which she often would pray back to God. I, too, have come to love them. Psalm 18: 28–29: *For you will light my lamp. The Lord my God will enlighten my darkness. For by You I can run against a troop. By my God I can leap over a wall,* and Psalm 34:7, *The angel of the Lord encamps around those who fear Him and delivers them.*

Chapter 5
World War II

Now to continue my story, which takes place during World War II.

It took many hours to travel back home on foot from the town of Tackmack where the Russians had attempted to have us all killed. When we returned home, many things had been taken out of our homes by the Russian people who lived among us in our villages. They knew that the Communists planned to kill us when they shipped us to Tackmack and did not expect us to return. So they raided our homes and took everything they desired. This made us very sad because they had been our friends. We managed to get most of our belongings back.

In 1941, the German army arrived in the Ukraine.

As we reached our villages the Romanian army advanced down the mountainside. Germany and Romania were friends and had fought against the Russian Communists. When we saw them we were so glad. At the same time, the German army came down the hill. Now we had our freedom again under the German occupation in the Ukraine where we lived. We could go back to our farms and eat from our own fruit garden.

I remember that first Christmas when we went to the Christmas Eve service. Each child received a small bag full of candy and chocolate. We could hardly believe our eyes that we had something so good to eat.

As we walked to church that first Christmas, the snow was falling softly and so quietly. We all remained silent and thoughtful. All the mothers were thanking the Lord God for the freedom to go to church and be under the sound of God's Word.

But it was so sad that all our fathers were gone and had been taken away by the Communists together with many young men. My father was not with us anymore.

For two years the German army fought the Russians. The Germans pushed forward toward Moscow, the capital city of Russia. But then something happened. The American army and their allies became involved and helped the Russian Communists because America felt that Hitler, the leader of Germany, was more dangerous than the Communists. Now the German army was weakened because they had lost too many soldiers and tanks. After two full years, the German army retreated. As they came close to our German villages, we were told to get ready and to leave our homes. We had twenty-four hours to get ready. A few men from the German military were assigned to control our villages.

Chapter 6
The Flight

On Sunday, September 12, 1943, we left our home in Russia. My mother found someone to help her kill a pig and some chickens. She cooked and baked all night long with my oldest sisters, who helped her. They packed the cooked meat in big pails. It took them all night to prepare the food. They were exhausted in the morning. The men in the village got the wagons ready. They put a heavy lined tent over the wagons to cover them. It looked almost as you see in Western movies with the exception that these tents were pointed. Everyone in all those villages packed everything in the covered wagons. Early in the morning my mother got us all dressed as warmly as she could because it was winter.

Our house was the last one in our village. On the other side of our yard was our neighbor, a mother with three children. She had two girls and one boy. Her husband and her sixteen-year-old son had been taken as my father had been, by the Communists.

When the German army came, they took my sister Tascha and other girls, who were forced to dig foxholes for the German soldiers so that they could hold back the Communist army. My sister Tascha was permitted to return home, but not our neighbor's daughter.

As we traveled toward Germany, girls were taken, including my sister Anita, to help out with first-aid work. My mother's heart was very heavy for our friend's daughter as Mrs. Thiessen and my mother were close friends. Again, God took care of my family.

Throughout the entire war, the Lord performed one miracle after another. We were separated so often from Mrs. Thiessen and her daughter, Helen, and over and over again we met each other. This was all just God's grace in caring for us. Mrs. Thiessen and my mother encouraged each other and prayed and often cried together.

I remember as we left our home for the last time, looking back and seeing our cats, a pig, some chickens, and other animals. It was hard to look back and leave everything behind. We loved our home and our orchard and garden. My mother cried and cried. She longed to receive word from my father and my one sister Helga who had left us such a long time ago. We had no idea what had become of her, since she left to live with Aunt Tina in Kazakhstan. But we had no choice but to keep moving forward toward Germany. The German army wanted us to keep moving so that we would not be caught between the two fighting armies.

We traveled for many hours in the horse-driven wagons. The wagon train was so long because of all the German people from all the villages that we could not see the end of it. We could not all ride inside our wagon at once because there was not enough room. So my mother and my four older sisters had to walk. Then we all took turns. Some walked while other rode and then we switched places.

After many hours of traveling, we were finally allowed to stop for the night. Each family had taken one cow along and some of the young women and young boys took care of them so that we would have some milk during the journey. Since all the older men and boys had been taken, these young people had to help wherever they could. There were with us, however, some of the men who had escaped from the Communists who helped to keep us moving.

Now we were allowed to get some rest for a few hours. That night something very sad happened. Two of the young men were assigned to keep watch during the night in a place made for that purpose. They were standing guard on that night. They heard a group of terrorists coming through this Russian village where we had stopped for the night. We do not know exactly what happened that night. But one of the young men must have shot into the air for some reason. The terrorists were riding in horse-drawn sleds because the roads were always covered with snow. When they realized someone was there, the terrorists turned around and killed both of the young men and then left the village. God in His great mercy again held His hand over all of us. Had the terrorists known how many German people were in that village they probably would have killed all of us.

The Russian people living in that village took us into their homes and gave us food to eat. We were all able to have a good night's sleep. It was with great sadness that we realized that the boys had been killed and all of us mourned with their mothers as we held a funeral for them. They were placed in a box, since we had no coffins for them. They were put into the ground and covered with some soil and we had to leave quickly because it was too dangerous to stay. We could not even trust the Russian people in the village where we spent the night. They too, might turn on us.

What a sad time that was! After the funeral service we continued our traveling without knowing what our future would be like.

Chapter 7
The Bitter Cold Winter

So we moved on, traveling through the snowy, bitterly cold winter days and nights. After many days we had to stop because our horses were very tired and we no longer had food for the horses. We never unhitched the horses from the wagons when we stopped to feed them because we always had to be ready to go. Whenever we stopped, one person from each wagon had to go together as a group to look for food and water for our horses. Often we would just feed the horses and give them water to drink and quickly move on.

Sometimes we stopped in an open field and rested for the night.

I remember being so cold. There was snow on top of our heavy bed covers. Two of my bunions had frostbite.

We had now been traveling for a couple of weeks. We began to hear shooting. The Russian army with the help of their allies advanced faster and faster, pushing the German army back. At one point the German army was preparing to hold up the Russian Communist army. They gave us food to eat and then told us to move forward. We could see the smoke from the shooting and the armies fought each other.

We traveled forward, always hearing the shooting from the tanks and guns behind us. We came to a big city and stopped there because our food supplies were gone. Some of our people from the wagon train went quickly into the city to see if they could get some food to eat. My mother and my oldest sister, Tascha, went. After they left we realized the Russian army with their tanks was getting ready to take the city. We had just crossed the Polish border. The Poles sided with the Russians because Germany had already taken over Poland.

I remember, as a little girl of perhaps six years old, praying that the Lord would help us through. Then my mother came running out of the city and told us she lost my sister Tascha. They had become separated from one another. My mother returned to the city again and Tascha came to us. Now my mother was gone!

Oh! Did we pray! And God heard our calling. My mother came back just as we began moving forward. That was a blessed time to see my mother at our side.

We had to cross over a bridge, which the Russians planned to blow up. Half of our wagon train made it across and the other half was left behind. We were among those who made it across to the other side of the bridge.

Now we were on our own because the German army had lost thousands of soldiers on the way from Russia to Poland. We drove further into Poland. The German army now occupied Poland and we were again taken care of by the German army. They took us and put us in Polish homes where the people were forced to obey the command of Germany. My mother's friend Mrs. Thiessen and her daughter, Helen, were still together with us. But now we were placed in Polish homes where they were forced to care for us.

I remember that my mother was very concerned about staying there. We, as Germans, might be considered their enemies.

All of us Germans from Russia now had to undergo a body cleansing because we had lice and other diseases from the lack of things necessary to prevent such things from happening and the conditions under which we lived.

After a month, because the German army was being pushed back into Germany we were told to leave Poland. We got ready and moved on toward Germany. Now the German army took some of the Polish men with them in order to get us to Germany. They took some of the little children in the closed wagons, which were called "buggies." A Polish man drove the wagon and others sat outside in front and on top of the buggy.

My sister Irma and I were placed in the buggy and off we went, with my mother and other sisters trailing behind us. The highways were crowded with horse-drawn wagons. All the German people in Poland wanted to get out as quickly as possible—some of us in wagons, some on foot. There were thousands of refugees.

It was here that we got separated from Mrs. Thiessen and Helen. It was mass confusion on the highways because there were no more German soldiers to lead us and we were all on our own again. My mother was afraid that she might lose my sister Irma and me and that is exactly what happened. My mother could not keep up with us and we became separated. The Polish people where we had been placed had taken our horses. They said they would replace our horses with better horses, but had lied to us. They gave us their old horses. All of a sudden Mother saw the buggy with my sister and me in it. Our Polish driver had stopped to feed the horses. My mother quickly removed us from the buggy.

She was so thankful to God to have us with her again. God had performed another miracle! My mother prayed her way through all these difficulties. We could hardly believe our eyes when we met up with Mrs. Thiessen and Helen, so we traveled on together again toward Germany.

Finally we arrived in Germany. We were so happy. It was a comfort to us to be there—but not for long!

Wherever we passed through, the Germans had left everything and fled toward the west. So we all drove further away from the Polish border. It was our goal to get away somewhere to the west where we might find the American army.

By now those old horses from the Polish people who had betrayed us had collapsed, and we were unable to go any further.

My mother, my oldest sister, and Mrs. Thiessen went to look for a place to stay. My mother was extremely afraid to do this since my sister Helga was somewhere in Russia, and my second oldest sister, Anita, had been taken away in Poland by the German army or Red Cross and we did not know where they were. Now my mother and six of us, together with Mrs. Thiessen and her daughter, Helen, remained.

Chapter 8
Germany

We found a place where we could stay. It was a bombed-out house which my mother, Mrs. Thiessen, and Tascha fixed up so that the wind would not blow through the house. All over Germany the houses had been bombed. It looked very sad.

Every day my mother, Tascha and Mrs. Thiessen would go and look for food to eat in those bombed-out homes. I remember once they found a big pail of thick syrup and some potatoes. So we ate potatoes with syrup and were so thankful to have some food to eat.

We were there only two weeks when the Russian army marched in. The Germans had surrendered and World War II had ended. We were right there when the Communist army entered Germany. Now we were in Russian hands again.

Oh! The hardship that came over us now is hard to describe.

The first two weeks were very hard. The Russians were wild and were permitted to do whatever they wanted. It was a very difficult time to live through, those two weeks. The Russians put us in barracks. Many soldiers would get drunk and they would go to houses looking for young women whom they took along for the night. They were raped. It was a difficult time for every young woman. Many of them tried to hide themselves or dress as older women, hoping that they would not be taken.

My sister was taken too. Oh! Did my mother pray and cry out to the Lord! Now that I am older I can understand how she must have felt. But God kept her strong in the Lord.

I remember one night we were all asleep in one small room. In the room next to ours were Mrs. Thiessen and her daughter, Helen. We heard a banging on the outside door. It was a drunken soldier. My mother told everyone to get up and jump out of the window and run. That is just what we did. But, to Mother's dismay, she realized my sister Margaret was left behind. So my sister Tascha ran back and got her out just in time. The soldiers broke the door in and captured Mrs. Thiessen and Helen. They dragged them outside and pointed their rifles at them. They threatened to kill them. Again, God was in control. He held his hand over them. Their commanding officer ordered them away and Mrs. Thiessen and Helen were allowed to go free. All the while this was happening we hid in a field. We heard the yelling and threats of the soldiers. We returned to the house. A few days later we all were put in one small room.

There were four families in that small room. I remember there were four beds, one in each corner of the room. One entire family had to sleep in one bed. We were pushed from barrack to barrack.

One night, all of a sudden, three soldiers came into our room. They were all drunk. My mother and her friend were praying, as always–quietly crying out to God for protection. One of the soldiers came to our bed where my mother and five of my sisters were sitting on the bed. My sister was lying on the floor, almost under the bed. Mother had covered her with a thick blanket. She was hiding from the soldiers. We had placed our feet on top of her body, pretending it was just a blanket for our feet. But then one of the soldiers made a remark and my mother knew that he realized someone was hiding here. But, again, the Lord protected us.

Another soldier tried to get to the woman in one of the other beds who had her children around her. The third soldier was so drunk that he was sitting on the other bed by the door, holding his rifle between his knees pointed at the ceiling. His gun went off and the bullet hit the ceiling instead of the woman. I will never forget how that shot sounded. That soldier had been playing with his rifle the whole time they were in our room. As soon as the shot hit the ceiling some of their commanding officers came and took the soldiers away. They put them in the cellar under house arrest because they had violated the restrictions placed on them.

The Russian soldiers took one of our young men who was disabled. He was forced to tell them where they might find young women to be used by them for the night. It did not take long and he would find out how he could go to homes where there were only older women. But then he was beaten for not leading them to young women. It was difficult for this young man to be used in this way.

Then we were put into a big theater room which was full of beds, together with many German families. My mother, six sisters, Mrs. Thiessen, and Helen remained together. Most evenings we sang together before we went to sleep. My mother told us Bible stories in the evenings. Here, also, too often the soldiers would come at night looking for young women.

One evening the people around us told us that we should sing every evening because they told us that they had noticed that when we would sing those good songs, the soldiers did not come to where we were. What they meant by "good songs" was that we sang Christian songs with a good message. Yes, God really did a miracle there among us. Those unbelieving people were listening to our songs and noticed that because of what we were singing, the soldiers left us alone. We never know who listens to us when we as believers praise the Lord Jesus Christ. We can be sure that God hears! How important it is for us as believers to live for Jesus and to be a blessing in this dark world.

Chapter 9
The German Lady

At one point my mother and Mrs. Thiessen made friends with a German lady whose name was Mrs. Frobel. She had two small boys. Her husband, who was in the German army, was missing in action. She had both her parents living with her. Mrs. Frobel and her parents all had typhus. My mother and Mrs. Thiessen took care of these three people who were so sick. Every day when they came home, they took a bath and changed their clothing in one room of the house and then came to us. Both Mrs. Frobel's parents died, but she got better. None of us got this disease. God protected us here again. Mrs. Frobel and my mother became very good friends. From this time on, we traveled together.

By now the Russian military had taken control over this part of Germany. Germany was divided into four parts. England, Russia, the United States, and France had each taken one part of Germany. We were in the hands of Russians again.

The Russian lieutenant who was assigned over us in this part of Germany was a very shrewd commander. My mother was ordered to care for the cows and their calves. At one point one of the cows was missing and the lieutenant flew into a rage. He took his rifle and held it in front of my mother and told her he planned to shoot her. My mother said that she had done everything she could and that there were no cows missing when she brought them in. They counted the cows again and there was none missing. God had performed a miracle again and protected my mother.

Her days and nights were spent in constant prayer. The lieutenant's wife found out that my mother could sew and so Mother sewed many clothes for his wife. In return, she gave my mother their leftover crusts of bread. We were so glad for those crusts of bread because there was butter left on top of them. My mother sewed in the evening because during the day she was given a better job because of the lieutenant's wife. Mother had to milk the cows, and this turned out to be a blessing for us. My sister Magdalen got very sick with rheumatic fever. There was no doctor for the prisoners. My sister became very ill and my mother was sure she would die. She had been responsible to care for Mrs. Frobel's boys, Irma, and me. Each day my mother secretly took two cups of milk because we had very little food to eat and no milk to drink. Magdalen, my sister, would drink those two cups of milk and God healed her.

Then we learned that we were put on the list to be shipped back to Russia. All the German Mennonite people were to be sent back. My oldest sister, Tascha, told my mother that she was not going back to Russia. After Magdalen got better, she started to sew backpacks in order to be ready to escape when the opportunity to do so presented itself, and that encouraged my mother. She was so happy that God worked things out here too.

Chapter 10
The Escape

Then Mother, Tascha, and Mrs. Frobel made plans to escape. Mother and Mrs. Frobel would go to the neighboring Polish city and find out how we could escape from the Russian occupation. They found out what time the military guard shift changed. It was at twelve o'clock, midnight. Mrs. Frobel and my mother would walk to the Polish city at night. They found a storeowner, a Polish man whom they befriended. He hated the Russian Communists. After a few nights, mother and Mrs. Frobel felt they could trust this man. He promised to help them escape.

Of course, my mother would not do anything without crying out to the Lord in prayer and this was again God's grace that they found someone willing to help us escape. For the next few nights, Mrs. Frobel and Mother did not tell anyone that we were Mennonites from Russia. It was forbidden to help any Russian Mennonites. Mrs. Frobel, who was a German citizen and had German papers, loved my mother and all of us because we were like her family and she wanted to stay with us.

After Mother and Mrs. Frobel had given the Polish man some gifts which were among the few valuable keepsakes she had taken with her from Russia, we found out that we were next in line to be shipped to Russia. The night before we were to be shipped to Russia the Polish man said he would get everything ready for us and that we should come to his store at midnight.

Everything would be ready for us! Mother and Mrs. Frobel came back to us at midnight at the time of the changing of the guard.

Each night when the guard changed, the new guard would go by our windows and tap on the window, at which time my Mother had to answer "we are all here." We had witnessed what happened to people who tried to escape. They were almost beaten to death. It was frightening to try to escape. We decided to try to escape in spite of the danger with God's help. The trip to the place we were to go took about twenty minutes to walk, one way. Mother and Mrs. Frobel had made the journey for a couple of nights. The guards never saw them. It was always a very trying time for us and also for Mother and Mrs. Frobel because we would never be sure we would ever see each other again. It was a dangerous thing to do. Again, God protected them.

Then came the last night. God gave us a moonless night at the right time. At midnight when the guard changed, the new guard tapped on our window. Mother called "We are all here." We were packed and ready to make our escape. As soon as the guard was gone we quietly slipped out of our barracks into the dark night. God had chosen the right night for us to escape.

Because there was no moon it was extremely dark. There were no streetlights anywhere. This was our only chance. The next morning we were to be shipped back to Russia, so we had to take advantage of the opportunity to escape. Mrs. Frobel had a small baby carriage where one of her boys was put because he was too young to walk that distance. We began our walk into town, terrified that we would be caught. We all walked quietly along the side of the road, always ready to jump into the field to hide if we had to do so. Then we saw a light coming toward us. It was a military jeep. It was our lieutenant with his guard soldiers coming back from the Polish city where we were headed. My mother grabbed my youngest sister, Irma, and me and ordered everyone to lie down in the field. Mrs. Frobel grabbed one of her boys and my oldest sister, Tascha, grabbed the other boy. The rest of us followed our mother's instructions.

The jeep passed us and did not see us. God again protected us. We got up and again hurried toward the city. We had to reach the Polish men who would help us. There were ten of us altogether. After midnight we came into the city and saw some guards. We had divided ourselves into three groups walking into the city. Some of us went on one side of the street and another group on the other side. The third group followed a little behind. This way we would not be noticed. But the police got hold of my sister and Mrs. Frobel. Another policeman came to my mother and said, "Don't worry, we know of your coming. We were told to get you safely to the store." The Polish man had informed the police about our coming. They had been sent to help us escape. But— could we trust them? My mother, Tascha, and Mrs. Frobel did not know if the Polish man would keep his word. Because the Germans had treated the Polish people so poorly, we were not sure he would not report us to get revenge.

God in His great grace used this man to help us. The man did not report us because God held him in His hands. Again, it was a miracle from God.

We were so thankful to be there but were still afraid. Again Mother prayed with us.

They gave us such a good supper that night and told us to go to sleep. He would awaken us at four o'clock in the morning and take us to the train station. He was the owner of a small grocery store. The next morning at four o'clock he awakened us and gave us food to eat. We were all packed into a small one-horse wagon. We did not believe we would all fit in that wagon since including himself there were eleven people. He packed everything on it and then brought us one at a time out of the house and into the wagon. Then he went around the wagon with a lantern to see if all was okay with us.

He instructed my mother to be as casual as she could when we would arrive at the train station. We were not to remain together as a whole group so that we would not be noticed. He told her that when he winked at her, she was to watch him. As soon as he would purchase the train tickets, he would walk away and my mother was to walk slowly after him. He would then give her the tickets while they pretended to be strangers talking together. All went smoothly. My mother had the tickets and the kind Polish man wished us all well. We all boarded the train and it slowly pulled out of the station. My mother told us not to speak "low" German and not to talk at all. We were to be quiet as possible. The Polish people would recognize our German language because we were German Mennonites from Russia. German Mennonites were forbidden to travel anywhere.

Chapter 11
The Roaring Furnace

As soon as we got on the train, there were two policemen who approached my mother and said quietly that they wanted two hundred zloty (Polish money) from them. They were suspicious of us. They told her if she gave them the money they would not report us. My mother gave them the money. It was all she had left. She had sold some of the bedding we still had from Russia and had found some money in the bombed-out house in Germany. We did not have much left anymore to sell or to give away. We had only two quilts and two pillows left. That was all we had left.

We now were traveling west. It was where we wanted to go. We had heard that the American army occupied West Germany. That was where we wanted to go. We wondered what had happened to my sister Anita. You remember that she was taken by the German army. She was to be trained to give first aid to the wounded German soldiers. We had no idea where she was. At that time Tascha, my oldest sister, would write notes to her on any pieces of paper she could find. She then dropped them into any mailbox she could find. We had no stamps or envelopes. She just dropped her notes into the mailboxes with no address. She always wrote where we would be. Before our escape we got a note from Anita which read, "Anita, Mother, cousin, come." That is all she wrote. It did not take too long for us to understand what she wrote. My mother had a cousin living in Canada. To us, Canada and America were the same. So that was what Anita wanted us to do. We were to come to the American Zone. We knew that the Americans were in the west and that was where we would make our escape. Anita had been taken over by the Americans from the Germans she served. We realized that God in His grace had brought Anita to the American zone.

After many hours of travel we had to get off the train. As soon as we came off the train the police surrounded us. The two men who had demanded payment had reported us.

We were ordered into a building. My mother prayed in her heart quietly. We were walked into a room where there was a long table on the back wall. The door was open. Behind the door in the corner was a metal stove with burning wood inside the stove because it was so cold. Three policemen were sitting behind the table. My mother stood in front of one of them and Mrs. Frobel in front of another of those men to be questioned. My oldest sister, Tascha, stood behind my youngest sister Irma. We all had long hair, which was kept in braids.

The room we had been ordered into was a small room. There were three policemen and ten other people. It was a very crowded room. They would not notice what my sister Tascha had in mind to do.

Justina pulled my youngest sister Irma slowly backwards to the stove behind the door, pretending to work on my sister's hair. With one hand she reached into her coat for our Russian papers, which were sewn into the lining of her coat. She had waited for the opportunity to get rid of them. Now she had a chance to do so. She removed them from her coat and threw them into the stove. That stove made such a roaring noise that the policeman who questioned my mother looked up and my mother looked back too. But God held the eyes of those three policemen. Again God protected us. My sister Tascha did not look up. She just kept working on my sister's hair. The papers identifying us as Russian Mennonites were burned in that fire.

The questioning of my mother and Mrs. Frobel took a long time. Mrs. Frobel had her German papers and we did not have any papers to identify us because Tascha had just burned them in the fire. We could not possibly give them the papers from Russia. They would have immediately sent us back to the Russian Zone and there they would have killed my mother and all of us. Mother told them that we were Germans and our papers had been burned in the bombing of the homes in Germany and we had lost everything. She told them that all we had left was what we had with us now. Mrs. Frobel kept telling the policemen that my mother was her best friend and my mother repeated the same thing. They both just kept on insisting they were best friends.

Mrs. Frobel informed them she wanted to go to the West because she had family there. She told them she had lost everything and that she wanted to take us along to live with her family there. Somehow they believed her and let us go.

All of a sudden they let us go and even gave us a horse and wagon. Two men took us into their wagon and drove us for a while and then told us to get out and that we had to give them a gift. My mother had no money left but they insisted that they wanted something so my mother gave them one of those two heavy quilts. Mrs. Frobel gave her gold watch, which her husband had given her. Now we had hardly anything left of our belongings.

We picked up our backpacks, which were now almost empty, and started to walk. Along the way Mrs. Frobel asked the people who we passed how to get to the American Zone. We kept going in the direction of the American Zone. When reached the gate where the American soldiers were, we were told to go back. No one was allowed in. That was a very sad moment for all of us.

Chapter 12
The Americans

So we turned around and looked for a place where we could make a home for ourselves. All around us were bombed-out houses. We took one of those houses. There Mother, Tascha and Mrs. Frobel fixed it up a little so that we could have some shelter from the cold. We remained near the American military that occupied that part of Germany.

Because Mother believed in being persistent she kept asking to be let in and did not give up. God's Word says that we should never give up. Mother had one of her most precious Bible passages that she held on to and she continued praying. That passage is Psalm 18:28–29: *For You will light my lamp. The Lord my God will enlighten my darkness. For by You I can run against a troop. By my God I can leap over a wall.* And Psalm 34:7: *The angel of the Lord encamps all around those who fear Him and delivers them.*

Again my Mother prayed that the Lord would see us through this difficult time.

We were told that without German papers the Americans would not let us into the American camp. So my mother went to the leader of the town and asked him to write us German papers. The first time she asked him he said "no." So my mother went day after day and asked him for German papers.

After a while he became very angry and told her not to come back anymore. So Mother really sought the Lord in prayer that God would soften this man's heart. She decided that with the Lord's help she would ask this man once more. She asked that the Lord prepare this man's heart. So for the ninth time she went to him. When Mother stood before him again, he looked up and then wrote her the papers for all of us and told us to go.

When my mother walked out she knew that God had answered her prayer. Yes, "With my God I can leap over a wall" just as God promised in His Word. She loved to depend on His promises in those difficult times. Mother, Tascha, and Mrs. Frobel headed toward the American gate. When they were still quite a distance away from the gate the soldiers lifted their hands indicating that they should get lost. They would not even talk to them.

Again Mother prayed and then took all of us along. We went day after day to ask them to let us into the American camp. Many times we walked that path to the camp and back. Then God performed another miracle. They let us inside. They said since we were Russian refugees, we had to be punished and put us in a bomb shelter with a great many people who had escaped from the Russian Zone too. To us, this was not a punishment. It was more like a little piece of heaven. We were treated so well and we got food to eat. We were so thankful that the Lord protected us through so many dangerous times.

We were in the bomb shelter for two weeks when the order came from the American government to ship all refugees over to the American Zone. The area where we were was a piece of land between the Russians and the Americans. It had become known as "No man's land." So the American government told the military to ship three trucks full of refugees to the west where the Americans were. We arrived at the American camp. We were there only two weeks and then were shipped to the American Zone in the city of Gronau, Westfallen in Germany. At this place there were many of our German Mennonite people, all of whom were refugees from Russia. Oh, how much we all thanked our Lord and Saviour Jesus Christ for bringing us all safely through. We were permitted to go to church. Children could go to Sunday School. What a precious time that was for all of us. We remained in the refugee camp in the American Zone in this part of Germany for about two years.

Chapter 13
Reunited

This is where my sister Anita came to visit us for the first time since our separation. She was engaged to a young man who was a Christian. They had never been in the Russian Zone but were sent to the Americans, where they had been treated very well. We were overjoyed to see her.

After two years we were sent to South America, to the land of Paraguay, a small country. Because Germany was divided up between Russia, America, England, and France, there was not enough land for all the German refugees from Russia to be sent to America.

Four ships containing German Mennonite refugees were to be sent to Paraguay. Only one ship at a time was to leave Germany. The ship that we were on was an American Navy vessel called the Heinzelman. The captain of this ship made a bet with another Navy ship captain that he would make it across the ocean in two weeks, and he did.

The American military was very good to us. The food was so good on that ship. My sister Magdalen and I ate everything on our plates and half of the food on my sister Margaret's plate, which she could not eat because she was seasick.

We were so thankful for what the Lord had done in our lives. He brought us safely through those many years of hardship which began before the war and during the war years. My mother truly lived the Christian life. She constantly pointed us to Jesus, who was the Lord of her life.

I will end here and share some Bible verses, which my mother so often depended on. I have come to love them too in my walk with the Lord. I have already quoted Psalm 18:28, 29 and Psalm 34:7 . 2 Timothy 4:7-8 says, "I have fought the good fight, I have finished the race, I have kept the faith. Finally there is laid up for me the crown of righteousness, which the Lord, the righteous judge, will give to me on that Day, and not to me only but also to all who have loved His appearing."

I thank my heavenly Father that He was always in control. He is now in control of my life and will always be in control.

Chapter 14
South America: Paraguay

The Mennonite people had formed an organization called the Mennonite Central Committee, MCC. This was an organization to take care of the Mennonite refugees in Germany who had come out of Russia from World War II. The leaders of the MCC were C.F. Klassen and Peter with his wife Elfriede Dyck. C.F. Klassen was the brother of Elfriede Dyck. There were more MCC leaders but I can remember only these three.

The MCC leaders tried to find a country that would accept the Mennonite refugees. They tried the United States and Canada, but neither country was interested. However, Paraguay in South America accepted all of us and even gave us land at no cost. The MCC leaders then had to find four ships to take all of us to Paraguay. The first ship was from Holland, called Vollendam, the second was from the Holland, called Heinzelman, and the third one was also from Holland, called Scharlstan-Monarch. The Vollendam made two trips to South America because it took four trips to get all of the refugees relocated.

The first ship to leave for South America was the Vollendam. I am not exactly sure how many days the trip took but I know that it was more than fourteen days. My sister Anita and her fiancé, Gerhard Wiens, were on this ship. Anita and Gerhard arrived in Buenos Aires, Argentina, in February 1947.

They were held up in San Lorenzo, Paraguay, because there was a war going on among the Paraguay people. The Mennonite refugees were kept in a camp for a year until the war settled down and a stable government took control. The president was a German, named Straus. He was a good man and let the refugees reign over their own affairs as long as we did not break any of the government's laws.

Anita and Gerhard, along with all the Mennonite refugees, boarded a train to San Lorenzo, Paraguay, on March 20, 1947.

Then they all traveled to Asuncion, Paraguay. From there they went on a riverboat, then a train, and finally by horse-drawn wagon, arriving in Chaco, Paraguay, at the Menno Colony on March 24, 1948.

Now back to Germany. Seven of us were still in Germany, my mother and six of us and my cousin, Peter Friesen, who met us in Germany and who came to live with us. He was one of those young men who was able to escape from the Russian Communists when they were rounding up all the young men. Peter's entire family was still in Russia because they got separated from one another. Peter was not married.

We had to wait in Germany because of the war going on in Paraguay. After a year, the war ended and we were brought to the ship at Bremerhaven, Germany, where we boarded the ship Heinzelman. True to his word, the Navy Captain had said we would land in Buenos Aires, Argentina, and 5,000 of us were now in South America. (We left Germany on February 24, 1948.)

From Argentina we were put on a train en route to Asuncion, Paraguay. It was a long ride and I do not remember how long it took to get there. This is where the president, his officials, and the whole army of Paraguay lived. Paraguay is a very small country in the middle of South America, with one big city, Asuncion. The rest of the country is very poor—a lot of small villages and a couple of Indian tribes.

From Asuncion we boarded a small riverboat, a very poor boat because we had to sit on the floor on top of our few belongings. It was hard to see so much poverty. From there we were put on a slow-moving train. Some of the young men in our group decided that the train was so slow-moving that they could walk faster, so they jumped off. However, the conductor saw this and said he would show them that the train could go faster than they could walk and so the men quickly boarded the train again. It was a long ride and the train moved very slowly. All we saw was wilderness, small trees, bushes full of thorns so that no one could get near the thicket for fear of getting caught up in it. There were no stores, no rest rooms, just gray bushes and sand. No asphalt or cement roads, nothing but wilderness. It was a very depressing and hopeless sight. which made it quite difficult for my mother to accept.

In addition to this, it was very hot in this strange country. We arrived at the end of the line. The train could go no further; there were no more tracks. As we left the train I remember my mother saying "Where have they sent us?" We were in the wilderness in all this heat. It must have been very difficult for my mother. To a nine-year-old, it didn't seem so bad.

As we were standing there a man came and asked if we were the Friesen family. When my mother said yes, he said "I'm here to pick you up and take you to my home." In a horse-drawn wagon we traveled many hours to the colony of Menno. These were the first Mennonite people who had settled there. They had come from Canada and had already lived there for about twenty-eight years when we arrived.

This village had only three farmers, with their land around them, surrounded by the bushy wilderness, sandy roads, and bitter grass the animals could not eat because of its bitterness. Everywhere was grass, growing in bunches to about a foot high, and in between was sandy ground. The sand was so hot that we could not walk barefoot.

We stayed with Cornelius and Maria Hander for eleven months; they were very kind to us.

The MCC leader had made an agreement with the Menno Colony people to take the refugees into their homes for a couple of months so that they could show us how to work on our land,

and they would help us build up our new colony, which was called Neu Land Colony of Chaco, Paraguay. It was a very primitive and different lifestyle.

The MCC had given these people money toward our expenses while we lived with them because they were very poor themselves and could not afford extra mouths to feed.

I learned horseback riding here and loved it.

Chapter 15
The Neu Land Colony

Cornelius and Maria Hander were not saved although they were religious and went to church. They did not know the Saviour personally. Many years later, in Canada, there was an awakening among the people in the colony and Cornelius and Maria Hander put their trust in Jesus.

After many months with the Hander family, we were moved to our Neu Land Colony. This colony had been founded one year before we came to Paraguay. Cornelius and his friend, who was his neighbor, and my cousin, Peter Friesen, went first to our new home colony and built a small shed, two walls with a grass roof. Then they came back and we all drove in the horse-drawn wagon to our new home in the colony, in a village called Gnadentahl.

Cornelius Hander stayed with us to help build our house. We all got involved in the building. First we got some kind of grass and cow dung and sticky soil and water, which we had to get from a place where there was some low land. Otherwise the ground was mostly sand, which we could not use. So we had a container made of wood with two handles, and in the middle was a spot for two bricks. First we mixed this messy mud together. We had a board on the ground, then we put this wooden frame on top of it and put the messy mixture into those two wooden forms. Then we carried it a little bit further into our yard, and set it down on the ground. Then we pulled the board underneath away and slowly lifted the brick form up, leaving two bricks from that messy mud. That's how we made bricks. It was a tedious process, which took about two hours.

The house we built had two big rooms. It had six windows for one room, two on each side and two at the end. The other room had the same number of windows, together with a roofed porch. The roofs of the houses had a type of grass dipped in mud which was put on top of the roof, a special long, hardy, firm grass, called schilf grass. This process had to be repeated every three years.

The roofs were always done with many of the young people from the villages. We helped each other that way. It was a real mess to make this kind of mud. Sticky soil, cow dung, and finely chopped grass and water were mixed on top of a wagon. In order for it to be completely mixed, one of my sisters and I would get on the wagon and into that mud with our bare feet and then walk on it until it was all mixed up. Then one of the men got on the roof. One had an axe, and some got on the wagon into the mud, and some would be at the grass bundles. They would then take a small handful of grass, and hand it to the people on the wagon, who would then dip it into the messy mud. Then they would hand it to a person beside the wagon, who then gave it to the person with the axe who then placed it on top of a tree stump to hack off a little of the end of the mud grass. Then he handed it to the person who would then throw it onto the roof for the roof man to stick it on the roof boards. It was a lot of hard work to get it all done. It took many hours to finish one house. After a while we got the other house up and finished too. Through all this my mother stayed close to the Lord.

The second house was one big room, the kitchen, with a small room for storage of the little food we had. We got two cows with calves, and two horses, a cat, and a dog from Cornelius Hander because they had been paid for that from the MCC (Memonoite Central Committee).

The cows did not give much milk because they would go out of our villages to look for food for themselves, although there wasn't much out there either. We did not have much rain. Sometimes it would not rain for three or four months.

I loved to ride our horses. I called the white horse mine and my youngest sister Irma called the brown horse hers. One day my mother drove the horse wagon to another village to visit some friends. When she came back, the white horse was not in front of our wagon, and mother told us the horse had died there. It had eaten some young bean leaves and there was something on them which killed it. That was hard for me to take because I loved to ride her with her very smooth back.

We didn't have much food. Everything had to be cooked or baked from scratch. Nothing could be bought. Our village, Gnadentahl, was one row of houses on one side and two houses on the other side at the other end of the village. We all had the land around our homes and across the road, the road that ran through our village. The street was very wide and sandy. Our yards were all just sand. We would always sweep and rake around our houses to make it look nice for Sunday.

We had three hectares of land behind and all around our house and three more hectares of land across the road. Of the land across the road, half was all full of bushes, thorny wild bushes that were very hard to touch.

Mother was a very hard-working person, so all my sisters and I had to learn how to work. I always loved to work in the field to make things look nice. I watched my mother and it's true that we inherit a lot of things from our parents. I'm so thankful to the Lord who gave me a godly mother, who taught us the ways of the Lord and did a lot of disciplining. She raised five young children without a father. The oldest three sisters were married at this time, although Helga was left behind in Russia. As I have already said, we did not know if she was married or even still alive at this time. Later we learned that she was married.

We would always get up very early in the morning, about five or six o clock, because by ten o'clock the ground would be very hot since it was so sandy. By twelve o'clock we had to stop working in the fields because it was too hot. Then we would have a very light lunch since we did not have much food to eat, and then take a little nap. We would go out in the field about three o'clock to work some more. About six o'clock we had dinner, again, a very simple meal. We could not go to a store to buy food. The only things we could buy were white flour (because wheat did not grow in Paraguay), salt, pepper, bay leaves, vanilla, and sugar (only white). This was all we could buy. We had to travel ten kilometers to the center of our colony. It took almost the whole day to make it when we had only oxen in front of our wagon. Then came the horse wagon; that made a big difference in time. Our wagon was very hard to ride in because we sat on a board on top of our side wall of the wagon. That board was put across sideways on top of our wagon, it was sort of detached on top of the wagon.

Chapter 16
Then Came the Horse and Buggy

Then came the buggy, such as they have in the Amish country in Pennsylvania. It was almost like a little bit of heaven; at least we thought so. We were so thankful to God for every little improvement we could call ours.

The Centrium, a bigger village where the leaders of our colony lived, was called Halbstadt. I think that village had two more extra streets, besides the wide main street. There the sawmill was built. The main parts were all imported from Germany in order to make the sawmill workable. The sawmill was needed to make the wooden boards that were needed to make beds, tables, chairs, and anything else that needed to be built. The furniture for our homes was made from wood. Our mattresses were sacks filled with dried straw.

We always had to look underneath our beds, under our bed covers or pillows, just everywhere before we could go to sleep, for fear that snakes or other creepy things could have gotten into our house.

Once I was driving to pick up my sister from the hospital on a Sunday when a big long black snake was crawling across the road. The horse stopped right there and would not move until the snake was gone.

My sisters Margaret and Magdalen worked in the hospital. I remember when our new building at the hospital was built, and the celebration for the completion of that beautiful building. Today we would call it a very simple building, a long one-story house full of rooms for the patients.

My sister Margaret, who was the cook there, had made a very simple meal for the guests: a Mennonite soup called borscht with oven brick white bread and some pastry for coffee time. When Margaret got up early in the morning on the day of the celebration, she found to her dismay that the soup was full of small ants. She was very upset and told her sister and they started to fish out all the ants from the borscht. They realized it would take them too long to do the job alone, so they called two more people to help them, but they did not tell anybody else of the problem. And so when all the guests came, we all ate the soup with the fresh bread and had a good protein meal because not all the ants could possibly have been removed.

We had two horses and so my mother made an arrangement with some people who had a male horse in order to impregnate our dark brown horse. That way we could get some young horses on our farms. This was done at two separate times and we had two more horses. Oh, how I loved that first baby horse. It was black with two white patched socks on the lower feet, and a white stripe on the forehead. Whenever I would ride the horse, the little one would walk in front of its mother. I had a long stick with which I would tickle its side and the little horse would take its back legs and hit the air. It looked so cute. I was teasing the little one and thought that it was very funny. It was, but I would not do it today. I was a teenager and did many things that were not right. That's why I'm so thankful that I had a mother who believed in disciplining her children.

My sisters, Margaret and Magdalen could not work on the land because Margaret, the fourth sister, had a muscle disease and Magdalen, the sixth sister, had a heart problem. Earlier in my story I told of Magdalen who was always doing good on the farm. One day she was running after one of our calves to catch it, but she had to stop and cough and blood came up. So my mother took her to the doctor for a checkup. Doctor Rackau discovered that she had a heart-valve problem. He suggested to my mother that she put her in the hospital and he would train her to be a nurse. So that's what my mother did.

After a while Doctor Rackau asked my mother if Margaret would also like to work for him and his wife in the hospital. That's how two of my sisters worked in the hospital. Margaret eventually became the cook for the hospital.

Now there were four of us left at home, my mother and three daughters. It was a lot of work for just the four of us. My youngest sister and I were still attending school. By now we were in grade four. I begged my mother to let me stay home to work on our farm because there was so much work. She finally consented to let me help her and Sonja. Later my mother told me how sad she was that I could not have stayed to complete the sixth grade, the highest grade at the village school in our colony of Mennonites.

I loved working on our farm but of course I also loved to play. I played with our baby horse, the calves, and the little chicks when they came out of their eggs. I built little cages for them to protect them from the big *habicht*, a big bird who would try to catch the little chicks for food.

We had to get wood to make the fire for the oven so that we could cook and bake. We had to drive into the woods with the horse wagon to gather the wood and take it home. One time, when my mother, Sonja, and I went for the wood Sonja sat on top of our wagon, which was full of wood. Our horses started to move forward and Sonja had no chance to lie down on the wood. Before she knew it, the horses had started and she was hit with a big branch from a tree. It was a miracle from God that she was not badly hurt.

Once we arrived home we had to hack the wood into small pieces in order to make a fire in the oven so that we could cook our meal. We had no electricity and we lit our house with lanterns. They always had to be cleaned and our pots and pans were black underneath from the burning wood.

There was one job I never liked and that was weeding. I really disliked it because it was a never-ending job. We all had straw hats with big wide brims in order to protect us from the hot sun.

I remember once that one of our cows had a calf. We wanted to find out where she would go, so we followed her into the woods, and Sonja said, "We better go back or we're going to get lost in the bush." I looked around and realized I did not know which direction we had come from. It was scary. I prayed quietly that the Lord might take us out of this bush forest and after a while we made our way out of the forest. It was an eerie experience. I remembered that two young boys from another village had lost their way in the bush forest, and that it took many people to find them. They finally found them after a couple of days, but the younger boy had died. The older boy was very near death, but the Lord gave grace and healed him.

Another time I remember, Sonja on top of the wagon again. My mother threw peanuts in the field on to our wagon and Kathe would put the peanut plants evenly all over neatly on the wagon. Then it happened. One of the peanut bushes that my mother had picked up and thrown onto the wagon had a snake in it. My sister quickly slid down from the wagon on the other side. Again a miracle from God, who protected her. We did not know which snakes were poisonous and which were not.

Chapter 17
The Horse I Loved

The first horse our horse bore was very small. When he was about nine months old he got sick and died. That was very hard for me because I had come to love this horse. I had to dispose of this dead horse. I took a rope and tied its back legs, then put the harness on its mother, and she dragged her horse out of our village. I climbed on top of the mother horse and rode out into the bushes far away, enough to leave the dead horse there. That's what we did with our dead livestock because the big vultures would eat the dead animals up in one week and only dry bones were left. I cried bitterly on the way back home. I was about twelve years old then. I was nine years old when we came to Paraguay and I was seventeen years old when we left for Canada.

We got another baby horse from the same brown horse. This one was light brown, very beautiful, and soon I loved this one too. Then we got two calves from our two cows. My sister Irma and I played a lot with our baby horses and baby calves in between working on the farm. When Mother would set a hen on about twelve eggs, we loved to play with the baby chicks after they hatched. We put a little cage around the hen. It was really precious to watch them start to pick a hole to get out. Irma and I would play with the first calves. I made a simple harness around their necks and a little wagon like a sled from wood sticks. Then we would teach them to go and pull that simple sled along. When the little chicks started to get small feathers on their little body, and the tail would start to grow, they were just feathers. I then would take clothespins and clip one on their feathery tails. It was so cute when they turned around in a circle that you would think they were dancing.

As the chick grew up I would take it into the chicken barn (a very small coop where I could barely stand up). I would put the chicks nicely on the chicken roads and they let me do that. They were sitting like soldiers all lined up in a row.

I remember the baking oven outside. My mother would heat it up with a lot of wood and then bake the rolls, bread, Napolis torte, and streusel küchen (crumb cake). This was about the only pastry we could bake there because we had a very limited supply of goods for baking and cooking.

Our main food from the crop was kafir. It looked almost like a corn stalk except there was only that big bunch of small white corn, like pepper corn except that it was white. It was as long as from my elbow to my hand and it was full of small white corn. This was the main food for our animals. We ground this white corn and it looked like dark flour, which we used for baking dark rye bread. We mixed it with our white flour and we roasted it for coffee; there was no caffeine in it.

I remember one Christmas my mother wanted to bake some cookies and a cake, but we had no white flour because it had not been shipped to Paraguay from Germany. I remember the whole cake just crumbled like a sand castle. It was a big disappointment for my mother and us.

However, God always gave grace to keep on living for Jesus and that's what my mother always did. How many times the Lord protected us there from the wild animals and snakes. I remember stepping on a snake twice but was not bitten. Another miracle from God. My mother had a sewing suitcase full of fabric and rags for sewing and mending our clothes. Once she opened it up and was about to take something out of it when a snake crawled around, but she was not bitten by the snake. Every village had some medicine in case of a snakebite.

One day, I remember, our female dog had puppies in our little barn, which was close to our house. One night she was barking and made such a loud noise that my mother went out to find out what was happening. There it was, a big rattler about two yards long and as thick as my arm. It had wound itself up as a wheel with its head in the middle raised and poised to jump at the dog. We could kill small snakes but this one was too big and strong for us. So we called our neighbor's son, who came and killed it. Not an easy job. A snake could only be killed by chopping its head off. I had no father or brother like so many of us, since they were all left behind in Russia. That's why we were dependent on the neighbor's son. She too had no husband but had three boys and four girls.

There were other kinds of food for us to eat. The Kafir, as mentioned before. Then there was the sweet potato, which looked almost like our white potato except that it was a light yellow color and sweet. Then there was the mandioca, which was like potatoes. It looked like a long thick root, and when you peeled the dark brown skin off you would cut it in pieces and cook it, either in gravy or fried. This was our food: sweet potatoes, mandioca and kafir. Our fruit was melon, almonchens, and watermelon, which were available only around the Christmas season.

You see in Paraguay the Christmas season is in the summer. Once a week we got beef for one meal.

Chapter 18
The Locusts

In the center village in Halbstadt was where they killed the animals for all the people of the colony. Therefore every village had to send one person with a horse wagon to bring the meat to their particular village. Then we had to cook it right away because we had no basement or any refrigeration; no way to keep it cool. The only cool thing we could ever get was the water from the well which every farmer had. The water from some of the wells was bitter.

My oldest sister and her husband lived on the other side of our neighbor and her well water was good for drinking, but we did not live close to each other. We had our own eggs and milk from our cows, but only enough to feed us. We did not get much milk from our cows because there was very little food for the cows to eat. We did not have any vegetables because the soil was sandy, although we had a little piece of dark soil close to our house. It was about the size of one of our bedrooms.

There we planted a little parsley and dill, and some cucumbers and some carrots. What we children did when we were hungry was to dig out some potatoes and eat them raw. Otherwise there was nothing to eat except for the three meals. We had planted the fruit garden close to our house but it would take a couple of years before we could eat fruit. We planted grapefruit, orange, and mandarin trees and guava.

From the guava trees we were able to pick fruit for us to eat, but it was only for the last two years that we lived there.

We had one teacher in our village for twenty-eight children. She taught grades one through six. My youngest sister Irma and I were both in grade two when we arrived in Paraguay. I was nine years old, going on ten, so that means I was ten years old in grade two, only because during the war years I could not go to school. So my sister Irma who was two years younger than I was in the same grade. This was the first time that we were able to go to school on a daily basis.

We never thought we would ever leave Paraguay, so when I was in the fourth grade I begged my mother to keep me home, especially since we had so much work on the farm. I loved to do all kinds of work. We built some fences with wire around our land. We could get the poles out of our bushes in the bush country and then we dug a hole, put the pole into the hole, and filled it with soil all around it. Then we would stomp with our feet on top of the soil to make it hard all around the pole. We had to get our wood for fire, all from the forest bush.

It was a small bush tree since we did not have any big trees where we lived. I remember once we had the hardship of enduring a locust cloud coming over us and we thought it was going to set down on our crop fields, except it did not. They kept flying further away because the first locust did not descend upon our crop. Had it settled down the entire cloud of locusts would have devoured our crop.

My sister Irma and I got on our horses and tied a long rope between our horses so we were riding side by side, except not close together but a couple of yards apart. The rope between us would wipe over our kaffir crop fields. We did this for a long time. Locusts are big and when they fly into your face it hurts. We had clothes with long sleeves and a tight cloth around our head to cover our hair and most of our face.

Then we had another hardship to endure. You see, when the locusts come they eat themselves full, fly into the bush forest, and lay their eggs in the ground. They dig holes in the ground and lay about fifty eggs in one hole. (There are thousands and thousands of locusts.) Then they die. After the eggs are laid, in about six weeks, they hatch and then the young ones come out of the hole. It was a very difficult time for the entire village. The big locusts are gray in color and the young ones are green. We were told to get ready for the young locusts. We all dug trenches in the ground as long as possible. They came from our end of the village but we had prepared ourselves as well as we could. Whoever could help was helping. We had put poison into the entire trench.

We stood in front of the trenches with all kinds of branches with leaves on them in our hands. Then we would try to hold them up when they came towards us so that they would fall into the trench filled with poison. Then we would cover the trench with soil in order for them to die. To no avail. More and more kept coming, covering our house on the roof, down the walls, and onto the outside oven. Mother was frying food there, but they kept coming. Of course some died there but they just ate everything in sight until they were full-grown. Then they flew away, but not before they had devastated the land. It reminded me of the plague in Egypt during Moses' day.

So we experienced the flying locusts, the hopping locusts, and a tornado that tore off some of our roof. But in all that, the Lord brought us through with His grace.

Chapter 19
Hardship in Paraguay

While in Paraguay, at the age of fourteen, I put my trust in Jesus Christ and accepted Him as my personal Saviour. At the age of sixteen I was baptized and accepted into the Mennonite Brethren Church, a Bible-believing church.

My second oldest sister Anita and her husband Gerhard Wiens decided to move to Brazil to accept a post as house parents in a missionary orphanage. This was very hard for us all, especially my mother. She loved the grandchildren, (they had four boys at that time). However, after two years they moved back to Paraguay. She was expecting her fifth child and did not want it born in Brazil. In the meantime my oldest sister and her husband moved to Canada. In order for them to move there they had to be sponsored.

It so happened that my brother-in-law's mother was our neighbor but she lived in Paraguay for two only years before immigrating to Canada. Of course my mother was sad because she felt it would just be a matter of time before my brother-in-law would also want to move. And that is exactly what happened. Tascha and Heinrich Pauls also went to Canada.

Now that I am a mother I can appreciate my mother's feelings. It's so much nicer if the family can stay together, especially as we age. This is something that you don't appreciate when you're young, but it is so important. Yes, I have done it too. I have told the Lord how sorry I am and repented and because He is a forgiving God I know I am forgiven and my sins are washed away. When He forgives, He forgets, and our sins are no more.

After Tascha and Heinrich had been in Canada for about two years, they asked us if we would want to come too. It would be so much easier for us since we were all females. It was very hard to keep the farm going. The ant killers would eat our crops and we had to plant over and over and over again in order to get something.

We did plant peanuts, which we really liked. It was another food to add to our meals. When the peanuts were ready to be brought in we took the plants to our small barn. We would put a big barrel in the middle and we would stand around the barrel each of us with one plant of peanuts, and hold the leaves tight with our hands. Then we would hit that plant hard over the barrel so that the peanuts would fall off the plant into the barrel. It was a long process and hard work until we got all the peanuts off the plant. Then we would put them out on the ground in our front yard, "Unser Hoff" in German.

Chapter 20
The Sand Storm

One day when Irma and I were home alone I saw something that I had never seen before. I could not see our neighbor's house which was much further away than in an American town. It was all gray, about one story high; it was a sandstorm. It swept across our village so that I could not even see our street, which was close to our house. It certainly was scary and we kept our eyes closed because everything was covered with sand, including our bodies from the top of our heads to the bottom of our feet.

A Wedding in Paraguay:
When my sister Tascha got married the young people of our village got together and made paper flowers because every guest would get a paper flower. The bridegroom would get a half-ring paper with a flower in the middle and two long streamers hanging down. The bride would get a green-leafed half-crown on the top of her hair and she would have in the back a veil hanging down, something like we have here in America, except a lot simpler. The guests would always come for lunch and the food was always lamb meat and borscht, a Mennonite soup, with home-baked white bread. It certainly tasted very good.

The weddings would last almost the whole day. In the afternoon we had coffee and rolls and Streusel Kuchen (crumb cake), all baked in our wooden oven. Mother would make the dough and we children had to bring some of the dough to a couple of neighborhood women who helped us bake the rolls and Streusel Küchen. The young people would always serve the guests at the dinner tables and then they would all sit together and play their string instruments and sing, all those songs with a good message. This was done after everyone had finished eating.

Those song times were always the best time of the wedding for me. I could never get enough of playing and singing with stringed instruments. I always felt homesick but now I know it was a longing for heaven.

Where we lived was called Chaco, Paraguay, and there were about four different tribes of Indians living there: the Guranees, the Scholopies, the Indians and the Morows. The Morows were feared by everyone. Their goal was to kill every white person; because their forefathers had been mistreated by some white soldiers, they called every white person an enemy who had to be killed.

After we had settled down there in our village some of our young men felt the call to become missionaries, and so began the telling of the good gospel news of Jesus to these Indians. After we left for Canada, many thousands of Indians became saved and followed Jesus, and today they live in houses, go to school, and have learned their own language with the help of our people. That's why God sent us to Paraguay, in order for these Indians to hear the gospel of Jesus Christ.

A little about the Indians who lived around our villages: They were usually dressed from the waist down with more or less rags wrapped around their waist. They would marry their girls off at the age of fourteen years, but they would never have more than two children. At first we did not know this, but then we found out what they did. It was very sad, but they did not know any better. What they did was kill the baby immediately after it was born by putting sand into its mouth and thereby choking it.

Another reason that God brought us to the land of Paraguay was so that the Good News of Jesus our Savior could be shared with those who had not heard.

Chapter 21
Canada

After much prayer and asking the Lord for guidance, Mother decided to follow Tascha too. My mother never made a quick decision because she did not want to do something without the Lord's will. So in the year 1955 in February, we arrived at the train station in Winnipeg, Manitoba, Canada.

It took us five days to get from Paraguay to Winnipeg. We took a plane from the village called Philadelphia in the colony of Fernheim, Paraguay. We arrived in Asuncion, the capital of Paraguay, a two-hour plane ride. From Asuncion we flew to Brazil and then to Miami, Florida; from Miami to Toronto and then a train all the way to Winnipeg. How different this was. It was hard to get used to this kind of weather and lifestyle. Oh, how I wanted to go back to Paraguay. I was so homesick I cried often. I was seventeen years old and if we would have gone back that first year, I would have been so glad.

I got married on August 6, 1960. My husband wanted to emigrate to the US. I got pregnant while we were waiting for our immigration papers. We moved to the United States in August 1964. My daughter, Viola Adam, was born in Holy Name Hospital in Teaneck, New Jersey. I had always wanted four children, but it was not the Lord's plan. I had four miscarriages after Viola. It was difficult but the Lord saw me through although I was not walking closely with Him.

We returned to Canada in April of 1965. We lived there for about six years, until February 1972. Because of so many hardships in my marriage, I left Ontario and moved back to Winnipeg with Viola. It was a big hardship to be lonely, disappointed, and full of self pity. I had no joy as a Christian. I was running away from God and myself and my family. I moved back to the United States looking for peace. I remarried, but I was still unhappy.

But God never pushes us aside, even when we make big mistakes and sin against Him. He still bids us to come to Him with all our pain and troubles. Yes, I went astray for many years, a driedup Christian. I had no joy in my walk with the Lord. From the outside, people might not have guessed it, but God sees it and He keeps pulling and pushing us until we get to the end of our rope. When we are ready to surrender all to Him, He then gives us what we can hardly believe.

My daughter Viola, too, has come to love the Lord now. She is married and has one boy. He was born August 26, 1995. I love that grandson so very much. He belongs to the Lord and I dedicate him to the Lord. My prayers are that my child will stay close to the Lord and my grandson Justin will walk with the Lord.

Yes, when I moved here from Canada I was all alone. Away from my mother, all my sisters, and all the friends and relatives I had there in Winnipeg, Manitoba, Canada. This was the place from where I could no longer run.

Chapter 22
The United States of America

I remember this so well. My mother and two of my sisters, Sonja and Magdalen, came to visit. It was one year before my mother died, at eighty-four years of age in 1982. They came for one week and we all went to New York City, to the Empire State Building. I stayed with my mother in the van and told my husband Karl to lock all the doors of the van. Karl, Sonja, Magdalen, Karl's daughter, Esther, and my daughter, Viola, all went up to the top of the Empire State Building.

As my mother and I were talking, she kept making the statement, "But I'm so glad that you are so happy." She repeated this many times. At that time I did not know that God had done something in my heart, but today I know that God had made it known to my mother that her many prayers had been answered concerning me. Her wayward child had come home to the Lord.

Yes, about two years after the Lord took my mother home to heaven, I came to know what it means to have joy in your heart, and what we can have in our Lord Jesus.

When we ask God for humility, in return He gives us Peace, all three. What I mean is, if we ask God for a humble, willing, repentant heart attitude, He will give us three kinds of peace. The whole peace with God, the whole peace with ourselves, and the whole peace with our neighbor.

Yes, the Lord has changed my whole heart and has given me so much joy and peace in my heart. It's all just grace from God: All the glory goes to Him, the Lord of Lords and King of Kings.

> Isaiah 26:3—You will keep him in perfect peace, whose mind is stayed on you, because he trusts in you.
>
> Philippians 4:6—Be careful for nothing; but in every thing by prayer and supplication with thanksgiving let your requests be made known unto God.
>
> Amen

Chapter 23
A JOYLESS CHRISTIAN LIFE

I HAVE BEEN ASKED from time to time, "Why don't you write more of your story and more about yourself. There must be more to your story!"

Going back to Paraguay, South America, when I was about twelve years young, I put my trust in Jesus. Here I would like to add to my story. On one Sunday afternoon I visited some of my friends and we were talking about all kinds of things when one of the girls asked me if I knew what being born again was all about. She asked if I had ever asked Jesus to come into my heart and into my life. It was then that the Holy Spirit convicted me that something was not right inside of me. She continued, "Would you like to know what it means to have eternal life and be ready for heaven?" Of course that's what I wanted more than anything else in my life. I did not want to make so many mistakes anymore. I wanted to be free of that guilt in my life, and not have so much fear of dying. So the friends asked if I would come along to our Sunday School teacher. When we arrived there she explained to me what it means to become a Christian. That afternoon I accepted the Lord Jesus into my heart. My younger sister and another girl also accepted Jesus into their hearts as well.

When I came home I shared my joy with my Mother and I asked her to forgive me for all my sins. I also went to my other sisters and asked for forgiveness because I always thought I was a very bad sinner. Of course we are sinners and need to repent and put our trust in Jesus.

Now I thought I would not sin anymore. Well, that soon changed. One day when our cow had a calf, my youngest sister and I had to hold it on a rope. I told my sister to hold it tight and don't let go of the rope. But somehow, she let go of the rope and I got angry and yelled at her. After a while, I realized what I had done by yelling at my sister and getting angry. I was so shocked and horrified at myself. How could I do that, as I am a Christian now? Christians don't do that, I thought. I apologized and asked her to forgive me. That was the beginning of a long life as a joyless Christian.

Whenever I did wrong, I always asked for forgiveness. But the evil one, who knows how to get us, wants us to be miserable. He uses anything he can to make us doubt our salvation. I asked God so many times to forgive me and help me not to sin anymore. You know, I thought that once you became a Christian you wouldn't sin anymore. I don't know where I got that idea. And, I thought, when I get older it will be much easier for me not to do wrong. Oh what a foolish thought it was. Our sins are worse and much bigger when we get older. What I did not know was Christians will sin and do wrong, but they can be forgiven and God will remember those sins no more.

When I was sixteen years old my mother sent me to a Bible School where we learned all about the Bible and its history. But my unhappy inner life as a Christian affected my studies in bible School. I begged my mother to let me come home, but she told me to stay and do my best. I was always afraid of our pastor visiting our home because he might ask me about my Christian walk and the Lord. I would not know what to say.

In the meantime, my older sister and her husband had already migrated to Canada. She kept writing us about how much easier life would be if we would come to Canada too. After a long time of my mother not knowing what to do, she finally decided to immigrate to Canada in 1955. The first year we were in Canada we were required to work and learn English. I worked in the kitchen of a Dutch Mennonite-run hospital. It was also this year that I met and started dating a young man. We enjoyed each other's company and he said he wanted us to be more than friends. The only problem was, he was not a Christian. I could have told him about the Lord Jesus. But not being a joyful Christian; I just ran away and broke off from him. Later, after I had married, I was told that he had accepted Jesus into his heart and he became a pastor.

After a while, I applied for a job as a nurse's aide at the Health Science Centre Hospital in Winnipeg Manitoba. But, I was told to come back after I had learned English. So I worked in a sewing factory, then a chocolate factory, while continuing to work on my English. Finally, in 1957, I got the job. Even with very limited education, only four years of elementary school, I was accepted to work as a nurse's aide at the hospital. I enjoyed my job very much. I also liked the people I worked with and made some good friends there.

One of the friends I made at work was a young mother with three children. She became a very good friend and invited me to her home and told me about a young man who played the German zither. The zither is a great musical instrument that stands on top of a table and makes a beautiful sound. It was at her house that I met Gottlieb. He had a love of music and he played other musical instruments besides the zither. I also loved music very much. He was a Christian and we dated for a couple of months. Then he asked me to marry him. Of course I said, "Yes". He was a Christian, and that's all that matters right?

Now, I was a joyless Christian. But I did not know that. There were so many things I did not understand or know about God's ways. Not every Christian is really living for the Lord, and not every Christian will fit together. We all have a human nature that plays a big role in our lives But, I did not think about all that before I got married. I just didn't want to be called an old maid, as some people like to do that. I always felt sorry for single women and didn't like when people would call them old maids.

The biggest problem in my life was feeling sorry for myself. I saw myself as being not so smart because I had so little schooling. I also did not think of myself as a good looking person. Someone once said the biggest mistake a young girl can make is when she cannot wait to get married. And, that's exactly what I did. In 1960, after some months of dating Gottlieb, we got married. My marriage was a very difficult life for twelve years. He wanted me to learn to play the zither musical instrument but I couldn't because I did not have the gift for that.

Early in our marriage, my husband had an aunt living not far from us. We would visit her and her family quite often. I liked them very much. I got along well with them, especially Aunt Ruth. Aunt Ruth's husband's sister, Ida, was married to Karl WIlmes. In1960, Ida, Karl and their daughter moved to the United States of America. A few years later Ida and Karl came from America to visit Aunt Ruth and her husband. Gottlieb and I visited witht them at Aunt Ruth's house and they told about their life in New Jersey, U.S.A. Ida talked my husband into moving to the United States. She told him he could have a very good job and earn more money there than in Canada.

During the first three years of our marriage, long before there was any talk about the United States, my husband and I were members of the German Baptist Church in Winnipeg, Manitoba, Canada. In just one year, my husband built up brass orchestra and stringed orchestra in the church. He loved music, but he could not get along with people. In the next year he tore it all down because he could not control his anger. And so when Aunt Ruth's sister-in-law talked about a job in the United States, he wanted to move there. I did not want to leave my mother and sisters behind; but, I gave in to him. I thought things might be better between us if I went along with Gottlieb. So we filed the necessary papers and eleven months later had our immigration papers and our green card.

On August 10, 1964, we set our for the United States of America. After three full days of driving, we arrived in Englewood, New Jersey. I was eight months pregnant with our first child. Aunt Ruth's brother-in-law, Karl, secured a job for my husband. However, Gottlieb got angry when he found out he would have a woman boss. He would not work for a woman. So he got another job, which he did not like. And, he did not like it in the United States. About six weeks after we arrived in the United States, our daughter, Emily, was born on September 27, 1964. Six months later, in March 1965, my husband decided to move back to Canada, but not to Winnipeg Manitoba. He moved us to Kitchener Ontario, Canada.

We made our home in Kitchener for seven years and during these years my life with my husband continued to get worse. I was afraid of Gottlieb's anger. The final year we were together was torturous.; I did not know what to do. I did not want to break up my marriage. I knew it was wrong, but feeling sorry for myself and being afraid, I took Viola and left for Winnipeg Manitoba where my mother and sisters lived. That was February, 1972. After a difficult and fearful twelve years of marriage, I file for divorce. I lived in so much guilt and heartache for the next five years.

Aunt Ruth called me and told me that her sister-in-law, Ida, had died in New Jersey. She went there after the funeral to tidy up the house and to sort out all the clothing and many other things because Karl did not know what to do with everything. When Aunt Ruth came back home, she called me and asked me if I could visit her. She told me that Karl would like to get to know me. He started calling me and soon asked me to marry him. So after a year, my daughter and I flew back to Englewood, New Jersey where I married Karl Wilmes on September 17, 1977.

But now having two step-daughters and my daughter to care for, life was not so easy. So my guilt was right back. But actually it did not come back, because it was always right inside of me. I could not run away from it. So I was tormented within my sould, with all that guilt. I wanted so very much to get rid of this guilt, but how? After a couple years of marriage, I went to talk to the pastor of our church. He at one point asked me,

"Well, Olga, what are you going to do about all of this?" I said, "I don't know." I remember this answer so very well. Karl was good to me. I just had a problem within my soul.

The summer Viola graduated from high school, my youngest sister and her family from Canada came to visit us. As we talked she asked if I would like to let Viola go to Bible School in Winkler, Canada. It was a two year course of just plain Bible School. I agreed to let Viola attend in the fall. That was September, 1982. At Christmas time, they had a Christmas program and invited all the parents to attend. Karl could not make it because of work so I flew by myself to Winkler, Canada to be with Viola at their Christmas celebration. My cousin and his wife invited me to stay at their house in Winkler after the Christmas program. I stayed with them one night then went back to my sister's house in Winnipeg. There, I got such longing to visit a couple of old friends. One was my sister's sister-in-law, Luise Wiens. The other friend, Mrs. Warkentin, was about my mother's age. As I visited Mrs. Warkentin, she kept saying, "But Olga, you look and sound so different. What has happened to you?" And as I visited Luise Wiens, she said, "But Olga, you sound so happy and so different. What has happened?"

When I flew back home to New Jersey, I realized something had happened to me. I had such joy and excitement within my heart. As I was thinking about this, I thought I should go to the pastor and tell him about this change.in me. All of a sudden, there was a war going on in my mind. I thought, "It's not going to help. It will be the same as in the past when I used to go forward in church to confess my wrongs. Even though I asked God to forgive me I could not let go of the guilt." But there was another persistent thought that I could not ignore, "Yes, go and talk to the pastor." And, that's what I did.

When I shared with Pastor Bill Kanutzen what I felt in my heart, he told me God has answered your longing and has heard your cry. He has done a great thing within your heart. Now share this with people you will meet in your life. Finally, I knew what forgiveness is. I received his forgiveness, his peace and His grace.

How many times had I cried out to God to forgive me, but I never had that whole peace that God's word talks about. I had a sin problem that was so heavy in my life. So many times I had grieved over all my past mistakes and I needlessly continued to carry that heavy burden of guilt.

Now all that guilt was gone and the joy of peace was there. God is a forgiving God. He wants to give us peace. That's why He sent His Son Jesus to die for us. All God wants us is to read his Word, the Bible, and to accept His forgiveness of sin through Jesus Christ. After that we should thank God often. That Him for grace and forgiveness, and for loving us until He takes the believers in Jesus home to heaven. Oh, how I thank our heavenly Father for what he has done for us.

> Psalm 51:10, "Create in me a clean heart, Oh God. And renew a steadfast spirit within me."
>
> 1 Peter 5:7, "Casting all your care upon Him, for he cares for you."

Chapter 24
HELGA'S EXPERIENCES IN RUSSIA

SHORTLY AFTER THE WAR broke out, Helga, together with her Uncle and Aunt and their family also had to flee their hometown. The Russians wanted all the German civilians away from the approaching German army. The Warkentin's, their children, and Helga were on the road for one and a half months both by train and on water. There was no possibility for personal hygiene, as they had no opportunity to change clothing. As a result, lice were a problem. They finally arrived in Kazakhstan, a soviet state about 4-5 thousand km to the east of their home village. Here they were each given a room and shortly after, Uncle Hans was sent away to a forced labor camp. Aunt Tina knit for others while Helga, at age 13, worked from 5 am to 7 pm as a farm hand, a very difficult job indeed for a girl her age. She had many painful hours of illness with rheumatism. She often could barely get up in the morning and then would walk with a cane until she was able to force herself to go on. How she longed and prayed for her mother during those times! Her pillow was wet with tears many a night.

In 1947, after the war, Uncle Hans was able to return. He decided to take his family to Karaganda, a city in Kazakhstan, about 2,000 km from their present location. Preparations were made and then Helga, because she was of a different household, namely Friesen, was not permitted to come along. She was left behind with great unwillingness and heartache.

During that winter Helga decided to follow her Aunt and Uncle to Karaganda without permission. Early one morning she packed her few belongings and left the village. With wolves howling in the distance, she knelt down in the snow, prayed to her God and started her journey to the nearest train station, about 12 km across the frozen prairie. There she had to hide until the train came, as Germans were not allowed to travel in the Soviet Union. She managed to board the train without a ticket and made it in one piece to her Aunt Tina's in Karaganda, no small feat without any personal identification papers.

It was in Karaganda that she met Hans Bergmann and they were married on December 4, 1949. Their first home was a house about 1.5m in the ground, 4m long by 3m wide. Walls were made of mud bricks and they consisted of straw mixed with mud. Usually when it rained it also rained inside their home! They started this dwelling with another family. In this home, Hans, Marichen, and Peter were born to them. Peter died after six months. Life was very simple and hard. They worked for the Kolchos, a state-owned farm.

In 1956 Peter was born and it was during that year that they received their first letter from Oma. How thankful and overjoyed they were to hear that their mother and sisters were alive and well! Life from here on it took on a new meaning for them with a new goal, that of being reunited with their family. How long would it be, before their new prayers were to be answered? A year later Otto was born, followed by Heinrich and Leni completing their family of six children.

Chapter 25
MY MOTHER'S HOME-GOING

My sister, Irma Janzen, told us sisters this story....

In spite of feeling ill, mother attended deeper life services held at her church in April 1983, just a few weeks before her home-going.

On Tuesday night, April 18, 1983, Gerhard and Anita's youngest daughter, Helen, was given a bridal shower by the family at Gerhard's brother's house.

Mother could barely walk but she came with my two sisters and seemed to enjoy the evening.

Her conversation was clear, and everything seemed fine.

The following Tuesday she collapsed, experiencing some temporary memory loss.

She was taken by ambulance to the Health Science Centre and was diagnosed with pneumonia. All family members were notified of her serious condition.

Olga came from New Jersey and spent that final week with mother and my sisters. On Wednesday night Hans and Margaret Neufeld visited mother, but she was asleep. The nurse asked them to try to wake mother since she had not had success in waking her up.

Several hours later, she awoke with peace written all over her face.

This peace was very evident as she shared with Hans and Margaret, the miracle which God had done in her final days.

Her fear of death was gone and in its place was joy. Just as Hans and Margaret had left, I came to see her. She shared with me the same thing that she was no longer fearful of dying. Then she said, "I am joyfully awaiting my eternal home."

Thursday I was at her bedside when she opened up; it was as if she was unburdening herself, knowing the end would come soon.

Mother talked about her grandchildren whom she loved so very much. She said, "it had been like two sets of grandchildren, the older ones in B.C. and the younger ones in Winnipeg.

She felt regret that she had not shared the Lord with the younger grandchildren as she had previously done with the older ones.

She also said, "Irma, you have not brought your children over very often."

I responded, "Because you have grandchildren staying with you for many years during your lifetime and I didn't want to burden you in your older years."

On Saturday she became restless and disoriented so I decided to stay with her for the night. First she talked in confusion as if we were all there with her. After some restlessness, she sat up and folded her hands as if to pray.

I asked her, "Mother would you like to pray?"

She responded by praying clearly and thanked God for her assurance of her salvation and prayed for all her family members wherever they happen to be.

Her concern had always been that all her family would stay true to the end and that no one would be left behind.

Many times in her life, she had expressed the hope that she would someday be able to say, "Here I am Lord with all my children you entrusted to me," and that was her prayer at this time, her condition was slowly deteriorating. Monday night she went into a coma from which she never regained consciousness.

The end came the next day. Early on Thursday morning her lungs collapsed, and she struggled for breath in the most dreadful way until evening when she breathed her last.

Tuesday, May 3, 1983, one week after she had been admitted to the hospital, she came through the valley and God took her to our eternal home. Thank-you God for taking my mother home, Redeemed by the blood of the Lamb, Jesus our Savior....

(My mother was 84 years old, Olga)

My Father & Mother and my three oldest sisters. 1930

Justina Braun

Fuerstenwerder
Mother's birthplace

Fuerstenwerder
Father's birthplace

1919 Johann Friesen

My Mother's school in 1976 Ukraine

The church in Ukraine

My father hid in this Building.

Left my mother.

Our street in Ukraine

Our flight from Ukraine

Mother and her sisters & brother

Mother & us sisters

Massive grave fifty bodies

our village in Alexanderwohl

Terrorists

Nester Machno – 1917-1918
Terrorist

Muslim Leader

Paraguay – 1954

Muslim – Terrorists on their Horses.

Paraguay

		Erwin Kroeker
		Mrs. Duester
		Willie Duester
		Kliewer/Reimer
		Abram Klassen
		Mrs. Bergen
		Jakob Dueck
		Mrs. Dueck
Heinrich Edieger		Mrs. Rempel
		Mrs. Warkentin
Church	Gnadenfeld Village – Colony Neuland – Chaco Paraguay	Goosen siblings
School		Mrs. Thiessen
		Mrs. Reimer
		Gerhard Wiens
		Wilhelm Loewen
		Heinrich Wiens
		Mrs. Martens (teacher)
		Mrs. Rempel
		Mrs. Ungar
Mrs. Reimer		David Unruh
		Mrs. Braun
Peter Froese		Mrs. Reimer
		Mrs. Pauls/Hecht
		Mrs. Friesen
		Heinrich Pauls

To be killed

Mother and five of us sisters

Concordia Hospital – Paraguay, South America – 1954

Olga (Friesen) Wilmes Paraguay

Magdalen in Paraguay 1954

My Mother, and all eight of us sisters, and Husbands.
Canada 1955

Mother & us eight sisters Canada

Sonja & Magdalen

Magdalen

Mother and five of us sisters

Karl & Olga and Esther & Viola

Karl & Olga's Wedding – 1977

Olga & Karl Wilmes

Olga

Karl

Olga

Karl, Carmen, Emily

Karl's 50th Birthday – 1979

Olga Wilmes

Karl & Olga

Viola

Viola

Justin

 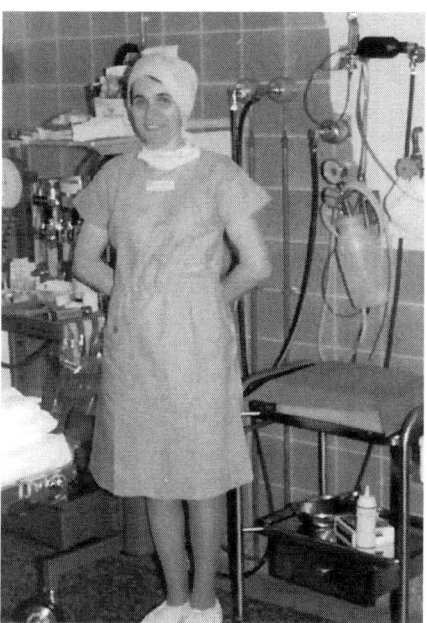

Justin   Operating Room Olga

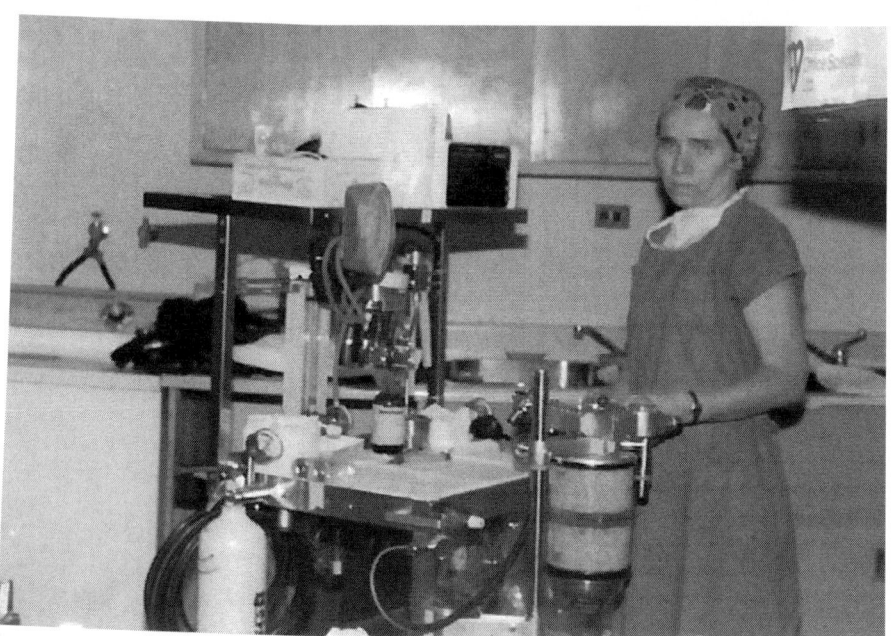

Anesthesia Operating Room Magdalen

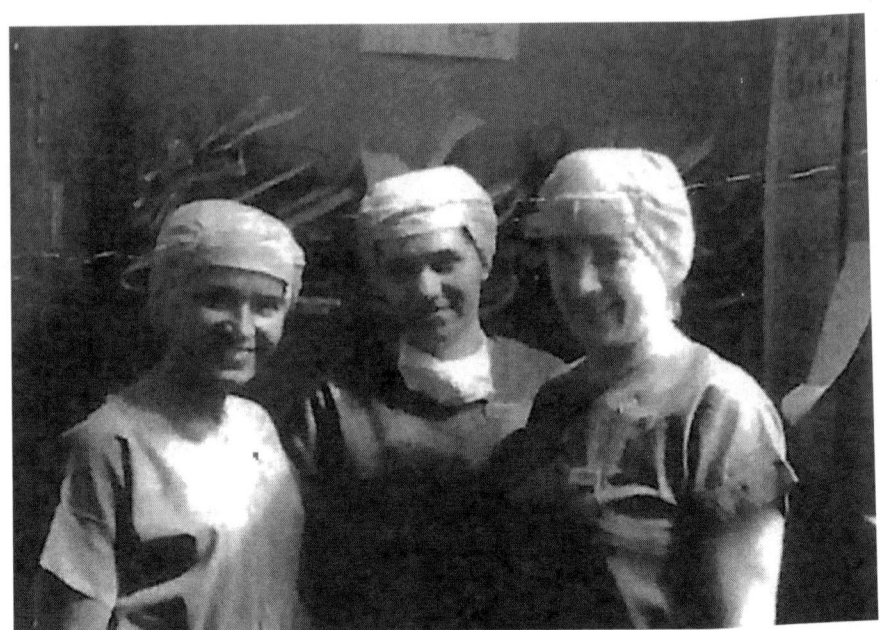

Anesthesia Olga's Friends

Olga & Friends 1958

Olga